Fish

by Helen Frost

Consulting Editor: Gail Saunders-Smith, Ph.D.

Consultant: Jennifer Zablotny, D.V.M.,
Member, American Animal Hospital Association

Pebble Books

an imprint of Capstone Press
Mankato, Minnesota

Pebble Books are published by Capstone Press
151 Good Counsel Drive, P.O. Box 669, Mankato, Minnesota 56002
http://www.capstone-press.com

1 2 3 4 5 6 06 05 04 03 02 01

Library of Congress Cataloging-in-Publication Data
Frost, Helen, 1949–
    Fish/by Helen Frost.
    p. cm.—(All about pets)
    Includes bibliographical references and index.
    Summary: Simple text and photographs present the features and care of fish
that can be kept as pets.
    ISBN 0-7368-0657-1
    1. Aquarium fishes—Juvenile literature. [1. Aquarium fishes. 2. Fishes. 3. Pets.]
I. Title. II. All about pets (Mankato, Minn.)
SF457.25 .F76 2001
639.34—dc21
                                                                              00-022988

Note to Parents and Teachers

The All About Pets series supports national science standards for
units on the diversity and unity of life. This book describes domesti-
cated fish and illustrates what they need from their owners. The
photographs support emergent readers in understanding the text.
The repetition of words and phrases helps emergent readers learn
new words. This book also introduces emergent readers to subject-
specific vocabulary words, which are defined in the Words to Know
section. Emergent readers may need assistance to read some words
and to use the Table of Contents, Words to Know, Read More,
Internet Sites, and Index/Word List sections of the book.

Table of Contents

4

Some fish are pets.

Fish live in water.

Fish are many colors.

Fish have fins.

tail

Fish have a tail.

Fish have gills.

Fish need clean water.

Fish need food.

Fish need room to swim.

Words to Know

fin—a body part of a fish that is shaped like a flap; fish use fins to swim and to steer.

fish—an animal that lives in water; fish have a tail, fins, and gills.

food—something that people, animals, and plants need to stay alive and grow; each kind of fish has a certain diet; some fish eat dry fish food, earthworms, and vegetables.

gill—a body part on the side of a fish; fish use their gills to breathe.

pet—a tame animal kept for company or pleasure; only certain kinds of fish can be kept as pets.

swim—to move through water; a fish swims by moving its body, fins, and tail.

tail—a part at the back end of an animal's body; fish use their tail to swim and to steer.

Read More

Coleman, Lori. *My Pet Fish.* All About Pets. Minneapolis: Lerner Publications, 1998.

Evans, Mark. *Fish.* ASPCA Pet Care Guides for Kids. New York: Dorling Kindersley, 1993.

Landau, Elaine. *Your Pet Tropical Fish. A* True Book. Chicago: Children's Press, 1997.

Schaefer, Lola. *Family Pets.* Families. Mankato, Minn.: Pebble Books, 1999.

Internet Sites

Fish Index
http://www.actwin.com/fish/species/fish.msql

A Home for Your Goldfish
http://www.acmepet.com/fish/library/goldfish2.html

Pet Care Tips: Fishy Waters
http://www.healthypet.com/Library/care-20.html

Index/Word List

Word Count: 34
Early-Intervention Level: 2

Editorial Credits
Martha E. H. Rustad, editor; Linda Clavel, designer; Jodi Theisen and Katy Kudela,
    photo researchers; Crystal Graf, photo editor

Photo Credits
Bill Losh/FPG International LLC, cover
David F. Clobes, 1, 6, 8, 10, 12, 14, 18, 20
Gregg Andersen, 16
International Stock/Bill Tucker, 4

The author thanks the children's section staff at the Allen County Public Library in
Fort Wayne, Indiana, for research assistance. The author also thanks Nancy T.
Whitesell, D.V.M., at St. Joseph Animal Hospital in Fort Wayne, Indiana.

24